D1740222

© Day One Publications 2009
First printed 2009

ISBN 978-1-84625-158-0
Scripture quotations taken from the
HOLY BIBLE, NEW INTERNATIONAL VERSION.
Copyright © 1973, 1978, 1984 by International Bible Society.
Used by permission of Hodder & Stoughton Publishers,
A member of the Hodder Headline Group.
All rights reserved.
"NIV" is a registered trademark of International Bible Society.
UK trademark number 1448790.

British Library Cataloguing in Publication Data available

Published by Day One Publications
Ryelands Road, Leominster, HR6 8NZ
TEL 01568 613 740 FAX 01568 611 473
email—sales@dayone.co.uk
web site—www.dayone.co.uk

All rights reserved
No part of this publication may be reproduced, or stored in a retrieval sys-
tem, or transmitted, in any form or by any means, mechanical, electronic,
photocopying, recording or otherwise, without the prior permission of Day
One Publications.

Designed by Kathryn Chedgzoy and printed by Gutenberg Press, Malta

Helen Clark

Simon Peter : Challenging Times

Pocket Bible People

DayOne

I am indebted to J. Glyn Owen for his book *From Simon to Peter* (Welwyn: Evangelical Press, 1985) for much of the material in this book.

Contents

'... Jesus still had work to do before Simon Peter would become the "rock"!'

Introduction: The story so far...

Before you start reading this book, you will find it really helpful to have made your way through *Simon Peter: The Training Years.*

In the first book we looked at:

- how Simon Peter first met Jesus

- how Simon Peter came to follow Jesus

- how Simon Peter was told from the very start that Jesus had a special job for him to do in building his church—such a special job that his name would be changed from 'Simon' to 'Peter', meaning the 'rock'!

- how Jesus slowly revealed who he was to Simon Peter and the other disciples, and that he had come to die and rise again so that his followers can join him in heaven when they die

- how the disciples, including Simon Peter, were pretty slow on the uptake but eventually worked out that he was the Son of God

- how the disciples, including Simon Peter, took even longer to understand the reason why Jesus had come, although it still hadn't quite sunk in

- how Simon Peter had a fair few lessons to learn, including humility and control over his words and actions.

This is a very brief outline but will hopefully remind you of where we have got to. We left Simon Peter after the Transfiguration, when he was probably feeling rather battered by one rebuke from Jesus and then another from God the Father. You would think that this must have been the lowest point in his training, but Jesus still had work to do before Simon Peter would become the 'rock'! Let's continue by looking at the challenging times that lay ahead for Simon Peter.

'... If God, who is perfect, can forgive us all our sins time and time again without end, who do we think we are not to forgive others when they ask?'

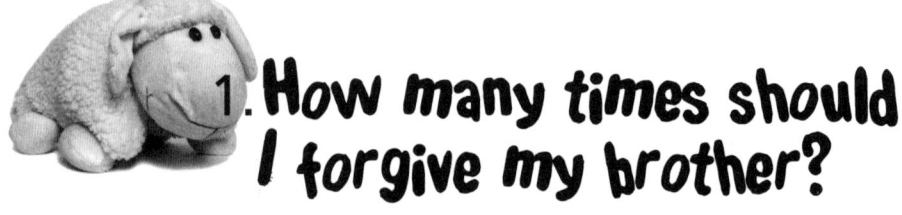

1. How many times should I forgive my brother?

Read Matthew 18:21–35

After the Transfiguration, the teaching continued. When you first read this passage in Matthew, you may think the subject is forgiveness, but I am tempted to suggest that, actually, pride is really at the root of it all. We looked

at this subject in the last chapter of *Simon Peter: The Training Years*, and the theme of pride seems to keep rearing its ugly head!

At the beginning of Matthew chapter 18, the disciples were wondering who was the greatest in the kingdom of heaven. This was a bizarre question to ask unless they were beginning to have delusions of grandeur and were hoping that Jesus would mention some of them in the top ten!

Jesus, of course, soon put paid to any ideas they may have had and stated that a person must become like a child in order to enter the kingdom of heaven. By that, he meant that people must be humble, assuming that others are better and more important than themselves.

Then, in verse 15, Jesus discussed what should be done if a brother (or sister, friend, etc.) sins against you (e.g. lies, cheats, steals, etc.).

It was now that Simon Peter asked the all-important question that I suspect the other disciples were all thinking too: **How many times should I forgive my brother (or sister, friend, etc.) when he sins against me (verse 21)?**

SIMON PETER TRIES TO SHOW HIS GENEROUS SIDE

You may look at this heading and think that I have finally flipped, but look at verse 21. Simon Peter suggested forgiving someone seven times, and this was actually a very generous suggestion.

The rabbis, or teachers of the law, were, in Jesus's day, well known for adding to the law that Moses received from God on Mount Sinai and one of their additions was that you should forgive your brother three times—that was all that was required. Why they came up with this number I have no idea, but as you can see, Simon Peter was being very kind by suggesting he would double the number recommended by the rabbis and add an extra one for good measure. He may have thought his suggestion would get him in Jesus's good books, but Jesus had another idea altogether.

SEVENTY-SEVEN TIMES!

Note: I do not for a moment think that Jesus gave this number expecting his followers to start counting the number of times they had to forgive someone and then stop at seventy-seven—that would be plain silly.

Jesus used this large number simply to explain that forgiveness is something that should never end. Whenever anyone asks us for forgiveness, no matter how many times that person may have asked before, we should always be willing to forgive.

• How do I know that Jesus meant there was no limit to forgiving?

• Why do we have to keep on forgiving all the time?

Have a look at the parable Jesus told, and all will be revealed.

ACCOUNT SETTLING!

A **parable** is a story with a meaning or a lesson to learn, and Jesus told many of these in order to get his points across.

Usually in a parable, the lesson behind the story was fairly obvious, and this parable in verses 23–34 was no exception.

Before you carry on reading, try to put into your own words what you think Jesus was trying to say in this parable.

To summarize this parable:

• A king was trying to settle his accounts with his servants.

• One owed him an awful lot of money and couldn't pay.

How many times should I forgive my brother?

• The king ordered him to be put into prison until the debt was paid (which would have been for an incredibly long time, as he could not earn any money while in prison).

• The servant begged for mercy.

• The king forgave him and cancelled the debt.

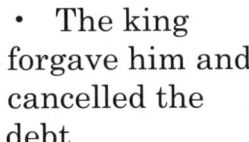
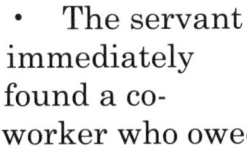

• The servant immediately found a co-worker who owed him a very small sum of money.

• He insisted the co-worker pay his debt.

• The co-worker could not pay and begged for mercy.

• The servant refused and had the co-worker thrown into jail.

• Other servants witnessed this and told the king.

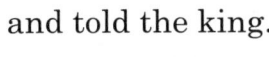

• The king was furious and reinstated the servant's debt, ordering him to be taken to jail and tortured for not showing the same mercy to the co-worker that the king had shown to him.

Message for today

And the moral of this story?

If we are Christians, God has forgiven us so much and continues to do so. We constantly sin against him, and yet he loves us so much. All we have to do is ask sincerely and he will forgive each time. Not only that, but he will wipe the slate clean so that it is as if we had never sinned in the first place.

That is something that, as human beings, we find very hard or almost impossible to do. We can forgive others, and we are called to do so, but we find it very difficult to erase the offence completely from our memory. Sometimes we will find ourselves being reminded of it and will bring it back into the open, where it has no place.

However, God does ask us to follow his example. If God, who is perfect, can forgive us all our sins time and time again without end, who do we think we are not to forgive others when they ask? By not forgiving others, we are suggesting that we are better than them, and that is a pride issue.

We need to be thankful that God is so loving and forgiving, and follow his perfect lead.

Don't let pride get in the way. We are all sinners and do not deserve God's forgiveness.

In fact, later in the New Testament we are called to consider others better than ourselves. So forgive your family, friends and neighbours unconditionally, as God has forgiven you.

Think tank

1. Think of a modern-day parable to put across this point of constantly forgiving. It may be a true story or one you make up.

2. Can you think of another story in the Bible in which someone had to be forgiven big time? If you are stuck, read the Parable of the Lost Son, Luke 15:11–24.

3. Is there someone you have to forgive, but you are finding it very hard to forget how much that person has hurt you? Ask God for the strength to forgive, and keep asking yourself, 'What would Jesus do?'

' . . . This life is not the end of the story. '

2. What do we get?

Read Matthew 19:16–30

I love Simon Peter for his honesty and the way he voiced what everyone else was thinking but was afraid to ask or felt was too rude to ask.

There he was in verse 27 asking Jesus what there would be for his disciples who had left everything to follow him. You can imagine the immediate silence there would have been among Jesus's disciples when they heard Simon Peter's question.

Some may have been waiting for Jesus to rebuke Simon Peter yet again for looking for a reward, as they saw it ...

But they all would have been listening intently to Jesus's reply, secretly glad that Simon Peter had been so upfront about the issue.

Message for today

This situation happens as often today as in Jesus's day. How many times have you been with your group of friends discussing how much allowance you all get and you realize you don't get as much as everyone else? Or why one boy got an extension on his homework and no one else did?

If Simon Peter was one of your friends, he would not waste time discussing it with you but would go straight to his parents and talk with them about a possible increase, or go to the teacher, probably in front of the class, and ask why that other boy got special treatment.

I am not saying it is always right to speak so boldly; there is a time and a place. However, it is no better to speak about these things behind people's backs. Sometimes going to the source can halt any further gossip or moaning.

Simon Peter would definitely be the one to get the record set straight and, on this occasion, Jesus was not cross with him for asking at all. He knew that Simon Peter and the other disciples had given up everything to follow him. He knew that they had sacrificed a lot and would continue to sacrifice and suffer for Jesus in the future. It was only natural for them to want to know it would not all be in vain but that there was something positive to look forward to.

But what prompted Simon Peter to ask this question in the first place?

THE RICH YOUNG RULER

To summarize Matthew 19:16–22: Jesus had just been approached by a wealthy man asking what he needed to do to get eternal life.

First, Jesus told him to obey the Ten Commandments. The man then assured Jesus that he had kept these.

Then Jesus struck at his weak point and told him to give all he had to the poor and follow him. I do believe that Jesus knew this would be the hardest thing for the rich man to do—and the man went away very sad.

Simon Peter clearly overheard this conversation, and you can imagine that his ears pricked up at this point and he was probably dying to interrupt Jesus to ask his question.

WAS SIMON PETER'S QUESTION A RESULT OF GREED?

My own personal opinion is that I don't think it was. Simon Peter did not ask what financial reward they would get, but simply what there would be for the disciples.

Remember, Jesus had spent time telling them they would suffer for him in the future and that the Christian life was not at all easy. It had been pretty depressing stuff. It was only natural they would want to see some light at the end of the tunnel.

I honestly think that Simon Peter and the other disciples truly followed Jesus because they believed he was the Messiah, the Son of God. They had seen his miracles and knew this man was special. They were not with him for what they could get, but it would obviously soften the blow of the suffering to come if they knew there was something positive at the end.

I believe Jesus knew that Simon Peter's question was not based on greed, and that is the reason why Jesus answered him openly, without any hint of anger.

Message for today

Just take a moment to think about this and try to put yourself in Simon Peter's sandals.

Just like him, we follow Jesus because we believe he is the Son of God, the promised Messiah. The disciples followed him because they loved him, just as we do.

However, although Jesus had warned them that he was soon to die and then rise again on the third day, I am not sure they had the benefit that we have of knowing that he died for us, in our place, so that we can be with him in heaven. I don't believe that, as yet, they had fully grasped the concept that he was to die so they could have eternal life.

Jesus's reply to Simon Peter's question soon set the record straight.

We should be so grateful that we have the benefit of knowing the full story and having it at our fingertips whenever we want. The whole truth has been revealed to us, but the disciples did not have the benefit of having the New Testament. We should be careful when we judge them, as I think that, if we were in their sandals, we would make many more mistakes than they did and get rebuked a lot more!

Note: Never take for granted the fact that we are freely able to read our Bibles at any time.

JESUS'S REPLY

Hopefully I am not going to confuse you too much, but I am going to look at verse 29 first and then go back to verse 28. I think it is important to look at the answer Simon Peter was wanting first, so bear with me.

'What will there be for us?'

1) Everyone who has left something or someone to follow Jesus will receive a hundred times as much (verse 29).

These words have, I think, been taken out of context far too many times. So many people like to understand them to mean that we will receive a hundred

23

times as much in material possessions—that we will be rich in this world.

If that were really the case, then why was it that Jesus and his disciples were so poor? There are some wonderful Christian people who don't even have two coins to rub together.

When will this happen?

  • I believe this will happen in the future once we are in heaven, where we will want for absolutely nothing.

  • I believe that it can also happen in the here and now, but not in a material sense.

If we call God our Father, then, as Christians, we are all one family. We are all brothers and sisters. So anyone who has had to leave family to follow Jesus can find comfort in having many brothers and sisters to provide support in the church family. In this way, you do receive a hundred times more family once you accept Jesus as your Saviour. I also believe you gain an incredible amount of peace and happiness from having Jesus as your Lord. Knowing he loves you and is watching over you is a comfort you don't have if you don't believe. Also, knowing that death is not the end is a wonderful thing. So from the emotional point of view, you receive a hundred times as much emotional comfort as you had before you believed.

2) Everyone who has left something or someone to follow Jesus will have eternal life (verse 29).

Eternal life is the most incredible gift that could be given to anyone. Most healthy people do not want to die, but the reality is that, unless Jesus comes again first, we all will at some point. What a wonderful promise that death is not the end and that we shall live on! Not only that, but we will be in heaven with Jesus, where there will be no crying, no loneliness, no pain. Nothing bad can happen to us there—it is going to be the most amazing, never-ending time, and I can't wait!

Would the disciples get special treatment?

If you look at the last part of verse 28, you will see that the answer is a resounding YES! The disciples will each sit on a throne and their role will be to judge the twelve tribes of Israel.

What are the twelve tribes of Israel?

If you look back into the Old Testament, in Genesis, you will read about a man named Jacob who was the grandson of Abraham. He had twelve sons, and this was really the start of the nation of Israel. Each son became the head of a group, or tribe, and every Israelite descended from one of these tribes. This was still the case in Jesus's day, so Jesus was basically saying that the disciples would judge the nation of Israel.

When will they start judging?

I suggest that this will occur once the disciples all get to heaven on Judgement Day.

The phrase 'at the renewal of all things' at the beginning of verse 28 suggests that this will all happen when Jesus returns to earth and evil is no more, but you could say it had already started once Jesus returned to heaven after his death and resurrection, as it was at that time that he once again sat 'on his glorious throne' (middle of verse 28).

Once Jesus had ascended to heaven, it would be the disciples' role to spread the good news of Jesus and to guide the new Christians and churches.

If you read some of the letters in the Bible after Acts, they are full of guidance on how to live and how not to live. What the writers of these letters said and preached came, we believe, directly from God, and in this way they had already started to take up the role of judges of the twelve tribes of Israel.

If I had been one of the disciples, I would have been quite stunned by now. Not only would they receive eternal life and a hundred times what they had given up for Jesus, but they would also become judges of the twelve tribes of Israel and sit on their own thrones!

I guess it was not quite what they were expecting, but I'm sure there were no complaints. These men—many of them lowly fishermen—would become judges of the whole nation of Israel!

No wonder Simon Peter had nothing more to say after that. Even he was speechless … for now, anyway!

Message for today

All Christians go through rough times when they feel that their faith is challenged and probably weakened. We can sometimes feel that the fight is not worth it, and lose sight of the reason for continuing.

If you are a Christian and you go through a period like this—which inevitably you will, if you have not already done so—take some time out and think about the following two points. I know this always helps me.

- Remember how much Jesus went through for you. He left all the comforts of heaven to come to earth, where he knew he would be put to a painful death on a cross. He did all this because of his incredible love for you.

- This life is not the end of the story. Yes, it is often a struggle, but once this life is over, we will be spending eternity with Jesus, where there will be no pain or sadness ... only happiness! It will be worth it, I promise!

Think tank

1. Had the rich man been truthful when he said he had kept all God's commandments? Which one do you think he was breaking by not wanting to give up his wealth for God?

2. Read Genesis chapter 49 to learn about Jacob blessing his twelve sons and the beginning of the tribes of Israel.

3. Have you had to give up anything for Jesus?

Maybe you have had to choose between your youth meeting and football practice or going out with your school friends.

As you get older, you will have the opportunity to go and see films or go to nightclubs with friends. Would you be prepared to give that up and say no if you knew that the film was not a good film to see or the club had a bad reputation?

These opportunities will come thick and fast as you get older. Remember, the disciples gave up everything for Jesus, including their homes. How much are you willing to give up for him?

' . . . For I gave you an example that you also should do as I did to you '

(John 13 v 15)

3. Jesus sets the example

Read John 13:1–17

This story marks the beginning of the run-up to Jesus's death. Jesus knew he would soon be leaving his disciples, whom he loved dearly.

From a human point of view, I would have been very worried about these men being left to cope without him. At this point, they really don't seem ready to take on the role of spreading the good news about Jesus to the rest of the human race—but Jesus knew that when the time came, they would be able to cope with the task admirably with the help of his Father and the Holy Spirit, who would come to them once he had gone back to heaven.

However, I am jumping ahead here! At the point we've reached so far, they were still a little clueless—not quite as clueless as they were at the start, but still not

getting the whole picture, as this story demonstrates.

One lesson they clearly hadn't learnt was humility and it was a lesson Jesus knew could only be taught by example!

THOSE DUSTY ROADS!

I don't know if you have ever ended up taking a walk with completely the wrong footwear. You think it is a lovely warm day so you wear sandals for your walk, but then find yourself on a very dusty path, and all the dirt and grime gets between your toes and under your feet. It feels very uncomfortable, and when you look down, your feet are a darker shade of grey!

Well, in Jesus's day, everyone wore open-toed sandals, and in Israel, the roads were very dry and dusty. After a journey, it was customary before a meal for the servant, if there was one, to come round the guests and wash their feet. Washing feet is obviously not the most pleasant of jobs, so it would naturally have been the lowest servant who would have been given this job.

NO OFFERS!

So there they were, with no servants to wash their feet. The disciples clearly had become a little proud during their time with Jesus and no one had taken it upon himself to do this lowly task. They must have felt it was beneath them.

Now the meal was being served and still the disciples were sitting there at the table with dirty feet.

You can imagine the scene and the thoughts going through their heads.

'I really think someone should offer to wash our feet, but I'm not going to do it—I am Andrew, one of the first disciples; it definitely shouldn't be me!'

'Well, I'm not going to offer—I was a tax collector once, you know!'

'It's not my place to do it—I was one of the three Jesus chose to accompany him during the Transfiguration. I'm too important to do something like that!'

THE LORD BECAME THE SERVANT!

What happened next must have made the disciples speechless ... again. Jesus got up and took off his outer cloak. He then wrapped a towel around his waist and started washing the disciples' feet in turn.

For example: Let's try to put this in today's terms. Imagine you are visiting Buckingham Palace in London to attend a royal Garden Party. Unbeknown to you, there is a staff crisis and all the staff have gone down with flu. There is no way any of them can serve today.

So there you are, walking through the front door, and you suddenly realize it is the Duke of Edinburgh offering to take your coat. Princess Anne is doing the guided tour, and out in the garden, Princes William and Harry are serving tea and sandwiches.

Well, you would have to scrape your chin off the floor.

Now, we all know that that is extremely unlikely to happen. In fact, I would dare to say it would never happen (although the princes do seem willing to roll up their sleeves when required), but it gives you some idea of how incredible it was to the disciples that Jesus would do such a thing.

Remember, these disciples now recognized Jesus to be not only a special man, able to do miracles and preach amazing sermons, but also the Son of God! This made the scenario even more jaw-dropping than the royal family acting as staff in the palace.

Simon Peter's reaction gives you some idea of how they all felt, but, of course, he put his foot right in his mouth yet again ... Will he ever learn to think before he speaks?

SIMON PETER REBUKED JESUS YET AGAIN!

I am sure that Simon Peter's reaction put into words what the other disciples were thinking. They started the following sequence of events:

• Simon Peter said, 'Is my Lord, the Son of God, going to stoop so low and wash my feet?'

• Jesus tried to reassure Simon Peter that he might not understand the reason now, but he would later.

• Simon Peter was having none of it!

• He said categorically that Jesus would never wash his feet! (I think that Simon Peter was suffering from a huge amount of guilt here. I think he regretted not offering to do the job before Jesus and couldn't bear the thought of his Lord kneeling in front of him.)

• He thought he was doing the right thing by refusing, but again he was going against Jesus and rebuking him. Simon Peter still hadn't learnt that you do not, under any circumstances, rebuke the Son of God!

• God's will is always done, and Jesus knew that stronger words were required now. He insisted that if he did not wash Simon Peter's feet, then Simon Peter would have 'no part' with him—he could not have any kind of relationship with him. There were no 'if's, 'but's or 'maybe's. It was a necessary requirement.

• I think Simon Peter was shocked, even devastated, at the idea of losing his relationship with Jesus. There was no hesitation in Simon Peter's response, but he did go a little overboard in then asking for the rest of his body to be washed, too. He loved his Lord and couldn't bear the thought of being separated from him.

THE SPIRITUAL BIT!

Read verses 10–11. Jesus's reply to Simon Peter's request for him to wash his whole body may, at first, seem a bit difficult to understand, but there is another element to this story that Jesus wanted to get across.

The idea of washing, or cleansing, is often used in the Bible as a symbol of making someone free from sin.

If you have ever seen a person being baptized, you will know that, in many churches, the Christian is led into a pool of water and lowered under the water briefly as a sign that that person's sins have already been 'washed away' and that he or she has a new life as a follower of Christ. Going with this theme, a 'full wash' is a sign of what happens when a person becomes a Christian and all his or her sins are forgiven and forgotten. People become Christians only once, just as they are only ever commanded to be baptized once. There is no need to be baptized again.

Hopefully, this will make Jesus's response a little clearer. Simon Peter was asking for a full wash but he had already given his life to Jesus when he declared him to be the Son of God. This full wash in spiritual terms had already taken place and there was no need for another one.

However, it unfortunately does not mean that, when we become Christians, we never sin again. We do, and we have to keep coming to Jesus and asking for forgiveness. We do not need the full wash time and time again, but we need what I like to call a mini-wash: the equivalent of just washing someone's feet, as Jesus was insisting on doing for Simon Peter.

Jesus confirmed this by stating that Simon Peter was clean (a Christian) and therefore did not need a full wash.

WHAT WAS JESUS'S REASONING FOR CARRYING OUT THIS TASK FOR HIS DISCIPLES?

Jesus explained why he did this in verses 12–17.

In a nutshell, he wanted to show them by example how they were to treat others; that they should be willing to serve whenever necessary, and in that way they would be blessed by God.

It is a matter of throwing away your pride. Never think you are better than anyone else. Remember, each person you come across, whatever state or situation that person is in, was created and is loved by God no less than you are. Treat everybody with love and respect.

Message for today

Just as the disciples were called to serve one another, so we are also called to serve. There is no room in the Christian family for pride, and no job is too basic for us not to take it up wholeheartedly.

When I was working as a nurse, there were times when I would be looking after a patient who was dying. When people are this weak, you have to do everything for them, including cleaning them once they have been to the toilet. Often, people, including family members, would ask me how I could do such a task. As a nurse, you have to study to degree level, and I do remember some nurses feeling that these jobs should be left to the care workers, considering them to be too menial for themselves.

However, I saw it as a privilege to serve another human being created and loved by God. I knew that, if Jesus was in the room, he would have no hesitation in rolling up his sleeves.

He calls us to serve one another and follow his example.

Think tank

1. Jesus did say that not everyone present was 'clean' (a Christian). Among those who were present, which person do you think was not 'clean'? (The passage gives a strong hint; see also Luke 22:47–48.)

2. I feel that Simon Peter was beginning to turn a corner with his pride issue. Look at his response to Jesus's rebuke in verse 9. Why do I come to that conclusion?

3. Have a think about how you can serve others.

Perhaps it may be something as simple as helping your mum with the housework or helping look after a younger brother or sister.

You could take any unwanted clothes to a charity shop.

You could offer to do some shopping or housework for an elderly person.

When you are older, you could volunteer to spend some time serving the homeless at a soup kitchen, or travel to a poorer country to help with building projects, etc.

The opportunities to serve are endless and you are never too young to start. Remember, at the same time you would be a wonderful witness for Jesus.

' . . . he was relying on his own strength, which would fail. '

4. Simon Peter learns a hard lesson...finally! (Part 1)

Read Luke 22:31–34 and John 13:33–38

In the next two chapters, we finally come to the best-known story about Simon Peter, the story that you will be most familiar with. Did you think we would never get there?

We are going to be moving around the four Gospels a little, but bear with me. Hopefully, by now you can find them quite quickly in your Bible.

LET'S RECAP!

Simon Peter had been following Jesus for approximately three years now, and during this time, there was one lesson that he seemed to have failed to learn. He did not listen and learn when Jesus told him some hard truths. He always felt he knew better than his Lord.

• He rebuked Jesus when he told Simon Peter he must die and rise again.

• He clearly did not get the point of the Transfiguration, and suggested something very silly.

• He rebuked Jesus when he was acting as an example and trying to wash Simon Peter's feet.

You would think that, by now, he would have learnt

that lesson and his pride would have been seriously dented, especially when, after the first incident, Jesus used very harsh words to Simon Peter. (If you need a reminder, look at Mark 8:33.)

There is no doubt that Simon Peter clearly loved his Lord and had the best intentions—I do want to make that clear. But he was not learning from his past mistakes and, unfortunately, this led to the biggest mistakes he could possibly have made.

Read Luke 22:31–34.

The disciples had just shared in the first-ever Communion, known as the Last Supper. During this meal, Jesus had again explained that he was to die and that one of his disciples was going to betray him.

What I find really hard to understand is how, after this very emotional time, the disciples could then have had an argument about which of them was considered to be the greatest!

Jesus interrupted them, and, in verse 31, he directed his comments to Simon Peter.

Note: Why did Jesus speak directly to Simon Peter? Remember, in Matthew 16:17–19, after Simon Peter had declared Jesus to be the Son of God, Jesus called him the rock on which he was to build his church. In other words, Simon Peter was to be the leader of the disciples in spreading the gospel far and wide after Jesus was gone.

FIRST WARNING

Jesus warned Simon Peter that Satan had been asking for permission to 'sift' the disciples 'as wheat'.

This may be a hard sentence to understand, but let me try to explain.

The word **'Satan'** means **'adversary'**—Jesus was referring here to the devil himself in no uncertain terms.

Message for today

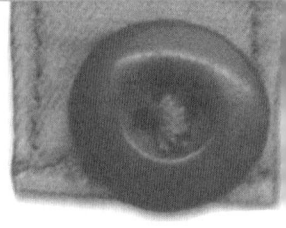

The devil is just as real as God and is someone we should never take lightly. He is not a cheeky character in a red suit with a forked tail and horns—someone you can laugh at; his only aim is to go against all that God does and try to turn people away from him.

Having said that, if we are Christians, we follow someone who is far more powerful than the devil, and as long as we keep our eyes fixed on Jesus, we have no need to be afraid.

Look at verse 31 again. 'Satan has asked ...' Satan has to ask for permission from God before he can have any involvement with us. I know it must be difficult to understand why God would give permission for us to be tempted by the devil and go through trials, but there is always a reason.

Although the devil's plan was to try to turn the disciples away from Jesus by sending these trials, the trials were essential in strengthening the disciples' faith and transforming their characters so that they could be used in a vital way by God.

Note: The phrase 'to sift ... as wheat' refers to how the farm workers, once they had gathered

grain, used a type of sieve to separate the good wheat from the unusable chaff (stalks, grass, etc.) that needed to be thrown away. Basically, Jesus was saying that the devil would test them to see whether they were devoted to him (wheat) or would fall away at the first hurdle (chaff).

Message for today

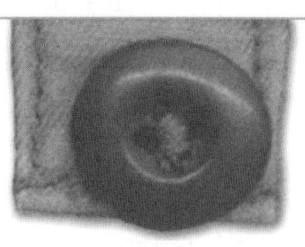

It is never easy going through hard times, but there is always a reason behind them. We don't always know the reason, but let me reassure you that there is one. When we go through these hard times, we must try to learn what God has to say to us and what we need to learn, and trust that God is moulding our characters so we can be more useful for him.

For example: My grandfather was a wonderful, faithful Christian man. Towards the end of his life, he became very frail and had to be nursed in bed, although he was able to stay at home. District nurses came to visit twice a day to help my grandmother, who really struggled to see him suffer so much. I also struggled with this; I couldn't understand why God was making my grandfather go through this and not taking him quickly to be with him.

It was only after my grandfather had died that I finally understood. The nurses who had looked after him came to visit my grandmother a few weeks after his death and they told her what an amazing witness he had been to them in his final few months, and how he had spoken to them of his faith and urged them to trust in the Lord. This had made a big impression on them. You see, even in his final moments, God still had work for my grandfather to do.

However hard some things are to understand, try not to question God, as he always has his reasons. We may sometimes never know what they are, but those reasons still exist.

From my situation with my grandfather, I learnt that as Christians we are never off duty until we join Jesus in heaven. No matter what situation we are in, God can still use us.

Read verse 32. Remember that Jesus will be praying for us in these situations, that our 'faith may not fail'. What a lovely thought: Jesus is as concerned for us as he was for Simon Peter.

Jesus knew that Simon Peter would eventually be strengthened in his faith because of the testing time that would come, and he would then be better able to support his fellow disciples—so there was a clear purpose to Simon Peter having to be tested.

SIMON PETER'S RESPONSE TO HIS FIRST WARNING

You would think that Simon Peter would have been so grateful for the warning and for the knowledge that Jesus was praying for him, but his response was arrogant and full of confidence in his own courage. It was almost as if Simon Peter was saying, 'Don't worry. I'm strong enough to cope on my own. Thanks for the offer of help but I can manage alone. In fact, I'm already strong enough to deal with anything that comes my way, even death.'

Simon Peter didn't realize that Jesus knew him far

better than he knew himself, and his response, that Simon Peter would have denied him three times by the time the cock crowed, proved to be true, as we shall see.

SECOND WARNING!

Read John 13:33–38. John recorded another conversation between Simon Peter and Jesus during this meal, and this was when Simon Peter got his second warning.

Jesus was warning the disciples that he would soon be going away and that they could not come with him this time. They were not to follow him. It was not their time yet.

SIMON PETER'S RESPONSE TO HIS SECOND WARNING

Rather than accept what Jesus had just said, Simon Peter immediately interrupted him, asking, 'Why?' (verse 37).

He was really like a small child.

For example: If you have any younger brothers, sisters or cousins, you will probably know that, whatever they are told, their answer is always to ask 'Why?' We were probably the same when we were young children. It is almost an act of defiance. They won't accept what has been said unless they are given a good reason that they can understand (especially if there is something nice for them at the end).

Well, Simon Peter was not accepting what Jesus had just said. He wanted a good reason as to why he couldn't come with Jesus. He felt he was ready for anything that came along, and felt so passionate about it that he would have been willing to die for Jesus if it was required.

Jesus knew that Simon Peter did not understand what he was saying and, however sincere he thought he was, that he was not really ready to make such a sacrifice.

Look at Jesus's response in verse 38: 'Are you really ready to lay down your life for me? I think not. You will prove me right by denying you even know me three times before the cock crows.'

If you look at the account of this incident in Matthew 26:35, Simon Peter even rebuked Jesus again after hearing Jesus's words, stating very strongly that he would never disown Jesus. What a fall he was about to take!

Poor Simon Peter. He was adamant that he was ready to fight for his Lord, and was very sincere about it; but he was relying on his own strength, which would fail. He also didn't seem to understand that Jesus had to die. By fighting for him, he was actually going against God's, and Jesus's, will.

Note: In Simon Peter's defence, you have to admire his honest intentions.

Message for today

If we learn one thing from this chapter, it is that Jesus knows us far better than we know ourselves. He knows our weaknesses inside and out, and our strengths, too.

Jesus kept trying to show Simon Peter where his weaknesses lay but he never seemed to learn and work on them. It took something awful, an event that would have made an impression on Simon Peter that he would never forget, for him really to learn his lesson—to listen to God, accept what he said, rely on him and not on his own strength, and to think before he spoke.

Listen to God when he is trying to teach you something. As you go through your life, learn from the mistakes you make. When you go through a rough time and come out the other side, look back and see what lesson you need to learn from it, and do learn from it. Don't keep ignoring what God is trying to say to you.

More often than not, my lesson is to rely on God and his strength rather than on my own strength—a similar lesson to the one Simon Peter needed, and one that most Christians struggle with, as I think we all have pride issues and need to work hard on squashing our pride.

Think tank

1. Why do you think Jesus reverted back to using Simon Peter's old name of 'Simon' in John 22:31–32?

2. Can you think of a story in the Old Testament in which the devil asks for permission to test one of God's followers? (Hint: the name of the follower has three letters, and the book containing his story is named after him.)

3. Often you may feel that you are going through hard times alone and that God does not feel very close when you are struggling. But if you are a Christian, he is right there with you, praying for you (even though you may not realize it).

A poem called *Footprints* is always a comfort to me in such times—you can read it on the opposite page. I always find it so reassuring to think that, when I feel all alone, it is not true. In fact, those are the times when God is carrying me.

FOOTPRINTS IN THE SAND

One night I dreamed I was walking along the
beach with the Lord.
Many scenes from my life flashed across the
sky.
In each scene I noticed footprints in the sand.
Sometimes there were two sets of footprints,
other times there were one set of footprints.

This bothered me because I noticed
that during the low periods of my life,
when I was suffering from
anguish, sorrow or defeat,
I could see only one set of footprints.

So I said to the Lord,
"You promised me Lord,
that if I followed you,
you would walk with me always.
But I have noticed that during the most trying
periods of my life
there have only been one set of footprints in
the sand.
Why, when I needed you most, have you not
been there for me?"

The Lord replied,
"The times when you have seen only one set
of footprints in the sand,
are when I carried you."

' . . . Before the cock crows you will deny me three times. '

(Matthew 26 v 75)

5. Simon Peter learns a hard lesson...finally!
(Part 2)

Read Matthew 26:36–54, 69–75

The time had come for Simon Peter to put his money where his mouth was (so to speak). He had declared that he would be willing to lay down his life for his Lord, but, when the time came and the potential threat was real, did he step up to the plate? Did he remain loyal to Jesus?

I think you probably know the answer to this, no matter how little or often you have had the opportunity to read your Bible, but let us go through the final moments up to Simon Peter's well-known denial, section by section.

THE SPIRIT WAS WILLING, BUT THE FLESH WAS INCREDIBLY WEAK!

Read Matthew 26:36–46. After the Last Supper, the disciples went with Jesus to the Garden of Gethsemane, where he was clearly upset, and told the disciples so, as he thought about what lay ahead for him.

Note: Remember that, although Jesus was the Son of God, he was also human. When he came to earth, he took on human form, which meant he felt pain and all the emotions that you and I feel. I can only begin to imagine how scared he must have

been, knowing he was about to be put to death in one of the most painful ways imaginable—nailed to a cross—never mind the torture he would endure beforehand, being whipped and having a crown of thorns pushed onto his head. And yet, if you can imagine it, this was only a small part of the suffering that lay ahead. Remember that the reason why Jesus had to die on the cross was because of us. He was willing to die in our place and take our punishment. To do that, he was going to have to take on all the sins of the world, including every sin you and I have committed already and will commit in the future. Jesus was pure and holy, yet he had to become our sin for us in order to pay the price we should be paying. The suffering he was about to go through is indescribable, and, to top it off, he would be separated from God the Father while he was going through this, as God cannot look upon sin. He knew that all this was ahead of him, and knew he needed time with his Father now to collect his thoughts and gain strength from the one person who could give it.

The disciples were made very aware of the fact that Jesus was in a great deal of anguish. So you would think that, if they truly loved him, they would have made every effort to have been there for him and supported him in his time of need.

But no!

53

Simon Peter: Challenging Times

- When Jesus returned after his first prayer session, they were all counting zzzzs.

- Jesus urged them to stay awake and keep watch.

- When Jesus returned after his second prayer session, they were back to counting zzzzs.

- Jesus didn't bother waking them this time.

- When Jesus returned after his third prayer session, they were still counting zzzzs.

The concern they had for Jesus must have overwhelmed him! (Note that I am being sarcastic here.)

Jesus must have felt very lonely at this point.

When you are going through a hard time, it is amazing what a difference support from friends and family can make.

For example: When you are taking an exam and are very nervous, it is always reassuring to talk about it with your friends or your parents and gain their support. Imagine if you came home after an important exam and your parents did not even ask how it went and showed no interest at all.

Or imagine if you were ill in hospital and absolutely no one came to visit you.

Jesus's situation was infinitely worse, yet his disciples, including the one who said he would lay down his life for Jesus, couldn't even stay awake for him.

Now I know that, late at night when you are tired, it is very hard to stay awake when you are praying, and I have failed in this area far too many times too, so I

54

know I am in no position to judge the disciples in this situation—but Simon Peter didn't really prove himself here.

Message for today

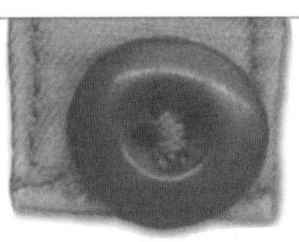

As I have just said, I do struggle to stay awake if I pray late at night, so I have stopped praying late at night when I am tired. I choose a time of the day when I am fully alert and less likely to drift off, and I recommend that you do the same.

Don't start praying when you are all snug and warm, curled up under your duvet. It is a recipe for disaster, and God is far too important not to give him your undivided attention. Try to pick a part of the day, perhaps when you have just got home from school, when you can devote some time to him. The prayers do not have to be long, but God loves to hear you pray, and your faith will benefit.

I know I have found that, if prayer takes a back seat, then, before I know it, my relationship with God is also suffering. Meeting with God regularly is vital—never forget that.

VIOLENCE WAS NOT THE ANSWER!

Read Matthew 26:47–54. Again, I have to defend Simon Peter a little here, although, as we will see, he was clearly in the wrong and not following Jesus's example.

It was late at night, and he had just woken up after probably a heavy sleep. He must have been feeling very disoriented—I'm sure you will have experienced that feeling.

Then, all of a sudden, armed guards appeared, and his fellow disciple, Judas, was betraying his Lord by leading them to Jesus.

It is at times like this, when your faith is not strong, that your basic instincts start to kick in. Simon Peter used to be a strong, burly fisherman and his strength was what he had relied on before meeting Jesus. His first instinct in this situation was, naturally, to fight back, and I think most people can understand and sympathize with this.

However, he was not taking note of Jesus's example. Jesus was not showing any resistance or argument but was willing to go with the soldiers without a struggle. Ideally, Simon Peter would have noticed this and realized that Jesus did not want any violence. But he didn't, and off came the soldier's ear.

Note: I can hear you asking how I can put this crime on Simon Peter when all it says in this passage is that it was 'one of Jesus's companions' who did the deed.

Well done if you did spot it. This is why it is always helpful to look at the other Gospel accounts to get their perspectives on the same story. So quickly skip to John 18:10, and you will see that the culprit is named as Simon Peter.

JESUS TOLD SIMON PETER NOT TO FOLLOW, SO SIMON PETER FOLLOWED...WITH DISASTROUS CONSEQUENCES!

If you look back at John 13:36, you'll see that Jesus had told Simon Peter not to follow him. It's a common problem among us humans. We are told not to do something, so we do it! Remember Adam and Eve? They were told not to eat from the tree of the knowledge of good and evil. So what did they do? Yes, they went and ate anyway, and that led to a whole sorry mess. Biblical history is filled with stories of people being told not to do something but disobeying, so Simon Peter was in good company when he decided to ignore Jesus's warning not to follow him.

Read Luke 22:54. It says clearly that Simon Peter followed ... at a distance.

There could have been two reasons why he followed at a distance.

> • He knew he was disobeying Jesus and did not want Jesus to know.

> • He was scared for his own life and did not want the guards to see him and capture him, too.

Either way, he seemed to have lost some of that amazing courage that he was quite vocal about earlier in the evening. Suddenly, he was not so brave.

SIMON PETER FAILS MISERABLY!

Now read Matthew 26:69–75. Here we find Simon Peter in the courtyard of the temple. From there, he would have been able to see what was happening. And it was here that he committed his final failure.

Three times he was asked by others in the courtyard whether or not he was a disciple of Jesus, and three times he declared he did not know the man. Each time, he was more and more adamant, until the third time, when he even asked for a curse to be put on him if he was not telling the truth.

I know that Simon Peter was scared. Everything had been happening so fast, he was on his own and he must have been scared for his life. We can have some sympathy for how he was feeling, and some understanding from a weak human point of view, but look at the contrast.

• Only a few hours earlier, he had been adamant that he was ready to die for his Lord and would never disown Jesus.

• Now, he had sworn three times that he did not know Jesus at all and had never met him.

What a fall, and what a change in attitude! This takes the saying 'pride goes before a fall' to a whole new level.

THE COCKEREL ENTERS STAGE LEFT!

Just in case you are not familiar with this term, a **cock**, or **cockerel**, is simply a **rooster**, or **male hen**. If you have ever spent time on a farm or deep in the countryside, no doubt you will have heard them crowing away as the sun is about to rise. In the summer, it can be particularly irritating, as they start crowing as early as 4 a.m.!

Anyway, once Simon Peter had denied Jesus for the third time, the cock mentioned by Jesus started crowing, and poor Simon Peter remembered Jesus's words.

We know he must have felt absolutely awful because this big, burly fisherman, who would have rarely cried at anything, 'wept bitterly' (verse 75).

This had ended up being a hard lesson for Simon

Peter to learn. You can imagine the further guilt he must have felt when Jesus was put to death and he thought he would never see him again.

Message for today

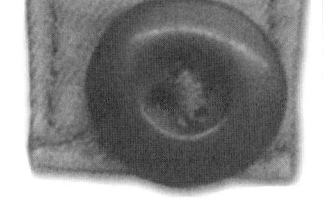

I urge you not to be too quick to judge Simon Peter. Most of us have never been in the position of having our lives threatened if we confess to being Christians. We are fortunate that today, in many countries, people have freedom to practise their faith.

The lesson we can learn here is never to rely on our own strength as Simon Peter did, and never to declare confidently that we will never do something. If we are relying on our own strength, we can fail at the worst thing imaginable if temptation comes along. It is only when we rely on God and on his strength that all things are possible, including standing up for Jesus in the face of a threat to our lives. There are many missionaries who have done just that because they were dependent on God for their strength.

If you look further on in Simon Peter's life, after he became a wonderful preacher for the gospel, you will see that there were many times when his life was in danger. He was imprisoned, tortured and eventually put to death, all because of his faith, but he stood firm and never denied his relationship with Jesus again because he was no longer relying on his own strength.

I can only pray that, if I am ever put in that situation, I will stand firm for Jesus, but if I do, it will only be because I am leaning on him alone and he is giving me the strength and courage I need.

I feel I must end this chapter on a lighter note, or you may feel utterly depressed. This is not the end of the story for Simon Peter, but really just the start of a new chapter in his life. He was now ready to change his character and work on those weak areas. He would soon be ready to be used greatly by God, so keep reading.

Think tank

1. Can you think of other examples of people in the Bible who disobeyed God's commands? Read:

- Genesis 18:1–15
- Genesis 19:15–26
- Exodus 32:1–35
- 1 Kings 11:1–6.

What did they do wrong?

2. How often do we deny Jesus, even when our lives are not in danger? Think back to times at school when you didn't admit to going to a club at church, or times when some of your friends were ridiculing Christian things and you didn't stand up for Jesus. Please be reassured that we have all been in those situations when, afterwards, we wish we had had the courage to say something but didn't. We are no different from Simon Peter.

Write down about a time when you did not stand up for Jesus, or when you had an opportunity to tell people about your friendship with him but kept quiet. Then ask God to forgive you and to give you the strength to say something next time. Keep on trying, and God will forgive you and help you. As we shall see, he forgave Simon Peter and never stopped loving him.

'. . . What a friend we have in Jesus, all our sins and griefs to bear!'

6. A new day dawns and things look altogether brighter for Simon Peter

Read Mark 16:1–7

The next two days must have been the darkest days for Jesus's disciples, especially for Simon Peter. They must have felt so lost without Jesus, and so unsure of what to do next. They were all in deep mourning, and, on top of that, Simon Peter had to deal with the guilt of denying Jesus in his final hours. It's a wonder he managed to get up in the morning!

But at the start of the third day, things began to look so much brighter.

Note: You and I both know that Jesus had told the disciples not only that he had to die but also that he was to rise on the third day. Whether they simply had not concentrated on the 'rising' bit after the shock of hearing the 'dying' bit, I don't know, but they clearly didn't remember his words and clearly were not expecting him to rise from the dead.

'GO, TELL HIS DISCIPLES AND PETER'

Three women came to the tomb early that third day to anoint Jesus's body. To their great surprise, Jesus was not there, but a strange man was. We are not told in this passage that this man was an angel, but two angels at the empty tomb are mentioned in John's account, in John 20:12, so there is little doubt that this man was an angel too, especially considering the special information he gave to Mary.

Jesus had clearly spoken with this angel about the message he was to give, and was very particular about Simon Peter being told. No other disciple was mentioned by name. Remember, Jesus knew that Simon Peter had denied him, yet he loved him so much and knew how guilty Simon Peter must have been feeling. He wanted to ensure he got the good news personally.

SIMON PETER MEETS WITH HIS LORD AGAIN!

Now, unfortunately, we are not told about that first meeting between Jesus and Simon Peter. Perhaps it was something just too private to share. The Bible only tells us what we need to know, so, clearly, this meeting was something we don't need to know about. We are only told about the episodes in which Jesus showed himself to all the disciples.

So how do we know that Jesus had this private meeting with Simon Peter first?

There are two passages that tell us they met.

• Luke 24:34. Jesus had just met with two of his followers as they were travelling to Emmaus. At the end of this meeting, the two men burst into the room where the other disciples were, and those disciples declared that Jesus's resurrection was true and that he had appeared to Simon Peter already. It was immediately after this that Jesus met with the rest of his disciples.

• 1 Corinthians 15:3–5. The letters to the Corinthians were written by Paul, one of the apostles who was a great preacher and teacher and who was used in a huge way to spread the gospel. He was not one of the original disciples but became a Christian after Jesus's death and resurrection, so was told about the events of the resurrection most likely from Simon Peter himself, with whom he worked closely. Paul stated that Jesus 'appeared to Peter, and then to the Twelve'.

How blessed was Simon Peter that Jesus chose to have a private meeting with him before he showed himself to the others! I have to be honest—I would love to have been a fly on the wall at that meeting, but we can all imagine:

• Simon Peter's utter joy at discovering that Mary had been right in declaring that Jesus was alive again

• his shame in confessing his sins and asking for forgiveness

• that there were more tears shed

• most of all, the relief on Simon Peter's face when he realized that the Lord had already forgiven him and still loved him.

Simon Peter would never be the same again. Satan had failed.

Message for today (1)

I find it so comforting and reassuring that Jesus is so quick to forgive and never stops loving us, no matter what we do. Hold on to that thought. No sin is too big that Jesus will not forgive you if you only ask and are truly sorry. He is that amazing! No friend you will ever have will be as forgiving as Jesus.

There is a very old hymn that you may know. I used to sing it often as a little girl, and I still read the words and find such comfort from them. Here is part of the first verse:

What a friend we have in Jesus,

All our sins and griefs to bear!

What a privilege to carry,

Everything to God in prayer!

Message for today (2)

Another important thing to take away from this passage is the thought that Jesus did not let Simon Peter go. Simon Peter had definitely gone through what we would call a time of backsliding, but he had given his life to Jesus, so Jesus was not about to leave him now. Jesus held on tight and specifically came to him to bring him back into a relationship.

Once we are Christians and have given our lives to serve Jesus, no matter how badly we fall, he will never let us go. He will actively look for us and will not rest until he has found us and brought us back into his loving arms.

For example: Years ago, I became friends with a girl who had fallen away from God in a big way. She had gone to Sunday school as a child and had made a commitment to Jesus, but she was seriously uninterested in anything Christian by the time I met her. She was still in touch with a few friends from her old church but was fed up with them constantly 'hassling' her about coming back to church. She thought her escape would happen when she went to university in London to do her nurse's training and that no one there would badger her about God.

However, God had other plans, and he was determined to bring her into his fold. It was a Sunday afternoon when all the nurses moved into their accommodation, and who was the first person she spoke to? Me! We got on quite well, and then she asked what I would be doing that evening. When my reply was 'going to church', she said afterwards that she couldn't quite believe it.

As there was nothing else for her to do, she came along with me. That was almost seventeen years ago, and now? She is attending Bible college and her faith is so strong.

Jesus would not let her go and used me to keep knocking on the door of her heart. She really had no choice but to let him in.

PREPARING THE DISCIPLES

Jesus was with his disciples for forty days before he returned to heaven to be with his Father. He spent this time teaching them, and this time they understood. They had changed.

Look at Luke 24:45. Jesus 'opened their minds so they could understand' the Bible. Up until now, they had been a bit clueless, but with Jesus's help they were now able to understand. Finally they were seeing the full picture and were almost ready for the big wide world and their next challenge of spreading the good news of Jesus.

A new day dawns and things look altogether brighter for Simon Peter!

Think tank

1. Read the Parable of the Lost Sheep in Luke 15:3–7. This will give you a wonderful example of how Jesus feels about his children and how he felt about Simon Peter. He will not give up until he has brought each of his children back into his fold!

2. Think back to when Jesus was teaching his disciples how they should forgive their brothers without limit—'seventy times seven'.

Here he was putting his words into action by forgiving Simon Peter so readily for something that I think you or I would really struggle with! Simon Peter must have really hurt Jesus, and yet, straight away, Jesus was there offering forgiveness. What an amazing example!

We must always remember to live the Christian life, not just talk it. We are often a better witness for Christ by how we act than by what we say.

3. Jonah was a man who was also called by God to be a witness. He was called to go to a place called Nineveh and warn the people there to turn to God and stop their evil ways. He wasn't keen at all and tried to go his own way.

- What happened when he tried to go his own way?
- What happened when he said sorry to God and obeyed his call?

PLEASE NOTE: I am not in any way suggesting that, if you fall away from God at some point and disobey him, he will cause you to be swallowed by a large fish! Jonah's experience was thankfully very unusual, otherwise there would be a lot of happy, full fish swimming in our seas right now! What I am trying to say is that God has a plan/a calling for each one of us once we choose to follow him. Once we have given our lives to him, he will never leave us. He may give us some difficult tasks to perform, but we never have to do them alone as he will always be with us, giving us the strength and the courage to carry them out. He will also always be ready to forgive us if we go wrong. Simon Peter had some very difficult times ahead to face, but God gave him the strength to stand firm and the wisdom to know how to act and what to say. He will do the same for us.

' . . . If we truly love Jesus, then we should be truly sorry. '

7. Simon Peter's future role is confirmed

Read John 21:15–17

Think back to when Simon Peter first confessed Jesus was the Son of God in Matthew 16:13–18a. Jesus told him that he would be used to build his church in the future. He was telling him of the role he was to play.

Many people use the word 'commissioning' to describe what happened then—this basically means that Simon Peter was called to and given this role by Jesus.

However, so much had happened since then, including, of course, Simon Peter's dramatic denial of Jesus. Simon Peter may have been wondering whether Jesus still wanted to use him in such a key role after he had failed him so miserably. Let's look through this passage and see what happened.

THE SCENE

We are still in the forty-day period between Jesus rising from the dead and returning (ascending) to heaven to be with his Father. He had just performed another miracle for the disciples—causing them to catch a huge number of fish—and they were all now sat around a fire beside the sea having breakfast (which Jesus prepared—he was still being a wonderful example to the disciples in serving them).

Jesus had clearly positioned himself next to Simon

Peter so they could have a private conversation. I truly believe Jesus had planned this to a T. The fire would have reminded Simon Peter of the fire in the courtyard outside the temple on that fateful night when he had denied Jesus, and I imagine that the episode would not have been far from his mind and that his emotions would have still been very raw.

Jesus turned to Simon Peter and asked him three times if he still loved him.

Each time, he used Simon Peter's true, full name. Simon Peter was in no doubt that Jesus was speaking directly to him.

FIRST QUESTION: 'DO YOU TRULY LOVE ME MORE THAN THESE?'

Read verse 15. Simon Peter would immediately have thought back to all his boasting about how he was ready to die for his Lord and how the other disciples might desert Jesus but not he. Effectively, he had said that he loved Jesus more than anyone else, with a love so pure that he was willing to die for him.

Well, he had been proven to have fallen short of this claim, so Jesus wanted to know where he now stood. Did he really love Jesus more than the other disciples, who were sat around the fire?

Simon Peter answered in the affirmative: 'You know that I love you.'

However, there are a few interesting things to note about his reply that make us realize how he had changed. He had examined himself and was finally speaking honestly and without boasting. Let's look further.

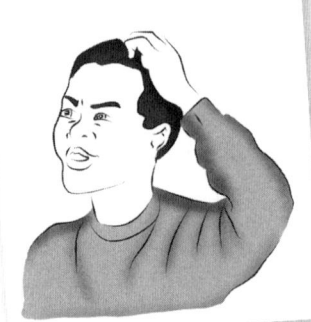
It's all Greek to me

It's all Greek to me

Don't get scared, but we need to look briefly at the original Greek language in which the New Testament was written. As I'm sure you are aware, the New Testament was not written in English, because no one spoke that language anywhere in the Middle East in Jesus's day. We have a gentleman called William Tyndale to thank for translating the New Testament so accurately into English for us a few hundred years ago.

Now, in the original Greek, there are a few words that can mean 'love' depending on which type of love you are referring to. In English we have only one word for love … and that, of course, is 'love'.

We need to look at which Greek word was used for 'love' in Jesus's question, and which Greek word Simon Peter used in his answer.

Jesus's word for love—agape

To put this as simply as possible, *agape* is the highest form of love you can have. It is a holy love, one that asks for nothing but gives everything, including one's life. It is a pure love—one that Jesus is surely capable of, but was Simon Peter? His boasting before the denial suggested that he was sure he was capable of such love and had such love for Jesus, but what about now?

Simon Peter's word for love—philia

In Simon Peter's reply, he confirmed that he did love Jesus but used the word *philia* for love, rather than repeating the same word, agape, that Jesus had used.

Why was this?

Philia is the word most commonly used for 'love' and it is a general term—the sort of love you would have for your brother. It is definitely not that high form of love that Jesus was talking about.

Basically, Simon Peter was determined not to be boastful any more, but to be as honest and thoughtful as possible. This was a totally new Simon Peter, one that had clearly been broken and had learnt some harsh lessons in the process.

His reply could read like this:

Lord, you know that I love you, but I cannot claim that I love you in the highest, purist form as I have not proved that to be the case. I have failed you and therefore cannot boast that my love is without fault.

It's amazing how looking at the original words can suddenly add an extra meaning to what seems like a very basic conversation.

SECOND QUESTION: 'DO YOU TRULY LOVE ME?'

Now read verse 16. No longer did Jesus ask if Simon Peter loved him 'more than these'. He was now just asking Simon Peter to examine himself thoroughly and answer again whether he loved him. Jesus again used the word agape in his question, and Simon Peter again responded in the affirmative but using the word *philia*.

He assured Jesus that he did love him, as much as he was humanly able to do, but he could not claim to love him with the higher, purer form of love that he once boasted of having.

I think that by phrasing it as 'you know that I love you', he was almost saying, 'If you think I do not even love you in this way, you must tell me I am wrong.'

THIRD QUESTION: 'DO YOU LOVE ME?'

Look at verse 17. Believe it or not, there was a significant difference in Jesus's question this time. He changed the word he used for love to the one used by Simon Peter— *philia.*

I think it is a sign that he appreciated Simon Peter's honesty and was coming down to his level.

Yet Simon Peter was very hurt by Jesus asking him a third time whether or not he loved him. It may have seemed to him that Jesus was suggesting he did not believe him, but I do not think that was the case.

You may not have noticed it, but remember that Simon Peter denied Jesus three times. To me, it seems that Jesus was asking for confirmation of Simon Peter's love three times in response to each denial.

Simon Peter's reply may have come out with a hint of frustration and perhaps irritation, but his words were utterly true and Simon Peter had come to realize this.

He replied with: 'You know all things'—and he does!

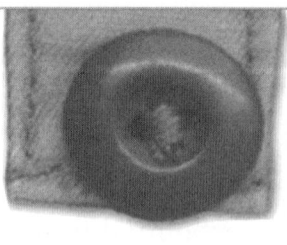

Message for today

Always remember that Jesus knows our hearts. When we have failed him and ask for forgiveness, he knows whether or not we are being sincere. He knows if we are truly sorry and, if so, will be happy to forgive us. He knew Simon Peter's heart and knew he would try never to be boastful again. I am sure there were times when Simon Peter failed, but Jesus knew that he loved him and that, in his heart, his intentions were sincere.

For example: When my brother and I were young, my father used to work in the town and tended to get home just before our bedtime. Whenever we were naughty, my mother always threatened us with: 'Wait till your father gets home and finds out how naughty you've been!'

Those words filled us with dread. My dad was (and still is) a very tall, strong man and, although very loving, when he was cross, you knew about it. There was nothing worse than the thought of him coming home and being angry with us.

As soon as that threat had been uttered, we would try anything we could to get back into our mother's good books, even to the point of offering to do the washing up. Every nice thing we did was followed by 'We are really sorry, please don't tell Dad!'

OK, so we were apologizing—but did we really mean it? Were we really sorry about having misbehaved and upset our mother? Sometimes we were, but I have to admit that, more often than not, we were just trying to avoid being punished by our father! We were not always sincere in asking for forgiveness.

I must also add that my mother mostly knew when we were being sincere and when we weren't, so we still got punished accordingly.

It is the same with God. When we know we have failed, we sometimes ask for forgiveness automatically just because we know it is the right thing to do, but we need to examine our hearts. Are we truly sorry, or, when the temptation comes along again, will we just give in again without a third thought?

If we truly love Jesus, then we should be truly sorry, because we know that we have upset him. Try to keep in mind that our main aim should be to try to please him in everything we do. Remember, if you are a Christian, Jesus truly loves you, and in the highest, purest sense of the word, as he gave his life for you!

JESUS'S RESPONSE TO SIMON PETER'S DECLARATION OF LOVE—HIS RECOMMISSIONING

With each reply, Jesus was confirming that Simon Peter still had a huge role to play. If he loved Jesus truly, then he could be used by him in his future role of building God's church. His future purpose had not changed.

Let's look at Jesus's replies to Simon Peter each time Simon Peter confirmed that he loved him.

- First reply—'Feed my lambs.'
- Second reply—'Take care of my sheep.'
- Third reply—'Feed my sheep.'

QUESTION: Who are the lambs and the sheep?

ANSWER: God's children.

Jesus quite often described himself as a shepherd and his people as the sheep—not literally, of course—and he carried on that idea here.

Again, it appears that he was simply saying the same thing three times, but if we look closely, we see that is not quite the case.

Feed and take care of ...

Jesus used both these phrases to cover all bases. He wanted Simon Peter not only to feed the sheep (i.e. teach people God's Word), but also to take care of them. He wanted Simon Peter to look after them from a spiritual and physical point of view, just as Jesus had done when he was on earth.

Remember, Jesus not only taught people, but he cared for them as well. He healed them when they were sick and fed them when they were hungry (e.g. the feeding of the five thousand). He taught by example.

Message for today

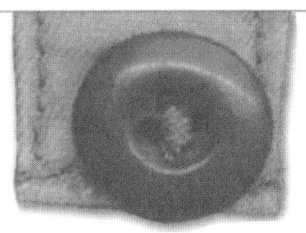

If we are Christians, we too are called not only to tell people about Jesus, but also to look after their physical needs where possible. It is no good trying to talk to hungry people about God. We need to feed them first, and then they will probably be more interested in hearing what we have to say. You will also have shown them by example that Jesus cares for them.

My lambs and my sheep ...

Jesus used both terms, lambs and sheep, to ensure no one was excluded. Simon Peter was to feed and care for young and old, black and white, and anyone in-between. There was to be no discrimination; the gospel is for all who will listen, and Simon Peter was to care for all.

Message for today

This commissioning was specifically for Simon Peter as the first missionary of the church, but if we are Christians, we have all been given the same role of looking after others and spreading God's Word to all, with no exceptions. Jesus came and died for all, and we need to take that to heart.

We will leave Simon Peter here for now. Jesus would soon ascend into heaven, but he did not leave his disciples alone. He sent the Holy Spirit to come and give the strength and guidance for their difficult road ahead as they took on this mammoth task. Simon Peter grew in his faith and in his knowledge and, with the Holy Spirit's help, he became one of the greatest preachers the world has ever known, as we will see. The good news spread rapidly and, with the aid of the other disciples and other followers of Jesus, the church of God was built. It was a hard road for Simon Peter, with many difficult times, and he was imprisoned on numerous occasions, tortured and eventually killed for his faith, but he stood strong to the end, as he was now relying on God's strength and not his own.

There is hope for us all!

This story should give us all hope. We often think we are too useless or not clever enough to be used by God. We may feel that we fail him time and time again, and why would he ever love us?

Simon Peter was pretty useless at the start and took three years of full-on teaching by Jesus to get to the point where he could be effectively used. He failed Jesus many times at the beginning, but God had a plan for him and used him in a wonderful way. He can use us too, if we let him.

Just like Simon Peter, we need:

- to love him
- to be honest with him
- to obey him
- to be ready to be used by him ...
- and Jesus will do the rest.

Don't make the mistake that Simon Peter made and rely on your own strength, thinking you know better. Lean on Jesus and he will direct your life.

Think tank

1. How can you start now to obey Jesus's command to feed his children and take care of them?

- How about finally asking your friend to come with you to the midweek group at your church?
- How about saving your loose change in a bottle and giving it to charity once it's full?
- How about volunteering to help in a younger section of your youth meeting?

These are just a few ideas, and I'm sure you can come up with many more. Remember, you are never too young to start caring for Jesus's lambs and sheep, even if you are only a lamb yourself!

2. In *Simon Peter: The Training Years*, I asked you to look at areas of your character that needed some work, just as Simon Peter needed to work on areas of his character.

For those who worked through the first book, how is that character assessment going? As you have been going through these studies, have you discovered a few more areas that perhaps need more work? I know I have! Don't get disheartened, but be encouraged. It means God is working in your life to reveal these areas to you.

Just ask for God's continued guidance and thank him for revealing these areas to you, as the first step is recognizing these weaknesses in your character. Only then can you start working on them.

Keep persevering! A friend of mine struggles with a bad temper and every day has to fight to keep it under control. Most of these weaknesses will involve a lifelong struggle, but God will be so pleased with you for trying.

If you haven't worked through *Simon Peter: The Training Years*, start examining yourself now for weaknesses in your character, e.g. a bad temper like my friend's, or lying, or selfishness. Start by asking God for help to change these areas, and keep working at changing them.

'...Prayer should always be a first resort, not a last resort.'

8. The Ascension

Read Acts:1:1–14

In our previous chapter, Jesus was still with the disciples, but the time had now come for him to return to his Father in heaven. He had done what he came to do.

You may have heard the term **'Ascension'** before. There is even a day in the calendar to commemorate this event. Simply put, it was the time when Jesus literally returned to heaven, and you can read about it in the first chapter of Acts.

Note: Acts is the book following the four Gospels in the New Testament. It documents the life of the disciples after Jesus had left and their struggles in starting the first churches and spreading God's Word. It may be a book you are not very familiar with, but is a fascinating read.

'DO NOT LEAVE JERUSALEM, BUT WAIT FOR THE GIFT MY FATHER PROMISED'

These were some of the last words that Jesus spoke to his disciples before leaving them.

What was the gift that had been promised them?

Look at verse 8 and you will discover that it was the Holy Spirit that would come upon them. (This was not news to them as Jesus had told them about the Holy Spirit's coming in John 16:5–11, before his crucifixion.)

So here is where we have to tackle one of the most difficult concepts in the Bible from my point of view—the Trinity!

THREE IN ONE!

Most Christians will try to avoid this topic if they can but it is important to have a basic idea of what the Trinity is, so I am going to try to explain it in simple terms.

First read 2 Corinthians 13:14. This book is the third one after Acts in the New Testament. The apostle Paul ends the letter with this verse:

May the grace of the Lord Jesus Christ, and the love of God, and the fellowship of the Holy Spirit be with you all.

You may have heard this verse before, as it is often used to end church services.

So far, you are, hopefully, happy with the idea of God the Father and God the Son. This verse explains their characters quite well. Basically, God the Father was so full of 'love' for us that he sent his Son, Jesus, into the world to die for us, which is a sign of Jesus's **'grace'**.

(**GRACE** = God's Riches At Christ's Expense. This is a handy way of remembering what grace means.)

So now we come to the Holy Spirit. Once Jesus ascended into heaven, he obviously did not want to leave his disciples and anyone who believes in him without guidance and help. This is where the Holy Spirit comes in. You will read about the Holy Spirit coming to the disciples in chapter 2 of Acts.

'**Fellowship**', in basic terms, means sharing and companionship. The Holy Spirit came to live in the disciples just as he comes and lives in each one of us when we become Christians, to encourage, guide, strengthen and give us power to do things that on our own we could never do. You will see what I mean when we look at how the Holy Spirit enabled Simon Peter to do all the things that are described in the next few chapters of Acts.

PUT YOUR THINKING CAP ON!

God the Father, God the Son (Jesus) and God the Holy Spirit are all God. Yes, they are individual and all have different roles, but they are all God (or part of the Godhead, as some people phrase it). Together, they make up the **Trinity**!

'Put your thinking cap on'

Split up the word TRINITY and you have TRI and UNITY.

- TRI means three
- UNITY means together as one.

For example: This is a really basic example and is by no means the best way of explaining the Trinity, but I know it helped me when I was younger.

Think of a clover leaf (the usual one with three leaves, not four).

A single leaf is made up of three leaves joined at the stem. Each section of the clover is a complete leaf, and yet together, the three leaves make one clover leaf.

So each part of the Trinity is God, and together they are the one God.

DON'T STRESS ABOUT IT!

The Trinity is a very difficult thing to really get our heads round and most adult Christians, if they admit it, struggle with the idea. Remember, there are always going to be some things that just baffle us about God. He is all-seeing, all-knowing and all-powerful. Our minds are tiny and we are not going to understand everything. However, we have been given enough knowledge from the Bible to believe and trust in him. As for the rest … that is where faith comes in!

BACK TO THE DISCIPLES IN JERUSALEM

Relax your brain for a bit as we are coming to the end of this chapter.

So Jesus ascended into heaven, and the disciples did as they were told and stayed in Jerusalem, waiting for the gift of the Holy Spirit.

I am sure they felt quite scared and lost at this point: scared that the Romans might come after Jesus's followers now, and lost, because their leader had left them.

And yet they continued to trust ...

The easiest option would have been to run for the hills, but they obeyed Jesus's final command to them and waited.

And they prayed ...

Read verse 14. They were all waiting in a room in Jerusalem with the women, but they did not waste their time making paper aeroplanes or playing I Spy. They did the most productive thing they could possibly have done, especially in a time of worry: they prayed! Jesus had taught them well.

Message for today

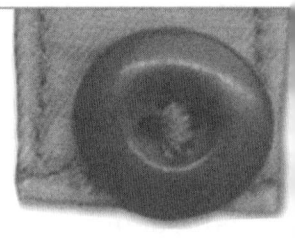

I don't know about you, but I have to confess that, when the going gets tough, the first thought in my head is not usually to get on my knees and pray. IT MOST DEFINITELY SHOULD BE, but, unfortunately, I confess it most often isn't.

I try to sort things out myself and then, when that doesn't work, I will suddenly think that maybe prayer would be a good idea!

Prayer should always be a first resort, not a last resort. We need to try to follow the disciples' example and have prayer in the front of our minds at all times. After all, God is the only one who can definitely help us in whatever situations we are in. It doesn't make sense for us to try to solve our problems ourselves first.

Think tank

1. Do you try to solve issues yourself first and only go to God as a last resort? Let's try to go to God first in everything. He really wants us to bring our worries to him and leave them with him. What an amazing privilege it is to be able to talk directly to our Creator! Let's use it!

2. In these books, I am asking you to look up different passages in various books of the Bible. If you are not used to looking things up in the Bible, try to familiarize yourself with where the books are. When we are in church, the person reading the passage will quite often give us the page number for that passage, but once the preacher starts his sermon, he will often skip to various passages to make his point, and then it is really handy to know which section to turn to. Otherwise you could get left behind.

When I was a child, my parents taught me a little song which recited all the books of the Bible in the right order. I am so grateful they did that, because I still sing parts in my head when I need to remember where to find books like Amos. Unfortunately, I can't teach you this song in a book, but spending some time going through the books of the Bible and working out where to find them will always be worthwhile. Maybe you can make a quiz with your friends to see who can find various books in the fastest time.

' . . . The Holy Spirit didn't waste any time working in the lives of the disciples. '

9. What a difference the Holy Spirit makes!

(Part 1)

Read Acts 1:15–2:15

When I read Acts 1:15–26, I am wondering where our proud, impulsive fisherman has gone. The Holy Spirit had still to come, yet Simon Peter was already taking up the role that Jesus had given him before he went away.

His small, eloquent speech in these verses doesn't resemble any of the words we have previously read from Simon Peter.

• Here is a man who sounds in control, confident, and as if he knows his Bible intimately.

• Here is a man who does not seem anxious about waiting for the promised Holy Spirit—he knows the Spirit will come at the appropriate time as Jesus promised—but in the meantime there is some work that can be done: choosing a disciple to replace Judas.

NO LEADERSHIP CONTEST

Remember that in Luke 9:46, the disciples had an argument over who was the greatest? Bearing this in mind, as soon as Simon Peter stood up and suggested filling that twelfth post that Judas had left behind, I would have expected a retort from one of the disciples in the vein of:

'Who put you in charge?'

... but nothing was said. No interruptions, queries, disagreements of any sort.

Verse 23 of Acts 1 simply says, 'So they proposed two men.'

They basically did exactly as Simon Peter had suggested.

Why do you think that was? I can think of a few reasons:

- They could not disagree with anything he said. He was speaking from the Old Testament and they could not dispute that.

- Simon Peter was a changed man and I am sure they noticed that. His speech did not have even a hint of self-importance or arrogance that could have rubbed one of them up the wrong way—he was just saying what had to be done.

- They were changed men, too. The whole episode of Jesus's death and resurrection had surely shaken them to the core. I would not be surprised if they were secretly glad that someone had stood up and suggested what to do.

- They would all have been eating with Simon Peter and Jesus by the Sea of Galilee when Jesus recommissioned Simon Peter and would therefore have heard Jesus's words and Simon Peter's reply. They were not going to argue with the Son of God again!

Message for today

As I have said before, I think that, if we are honest with ourselves, we know that we all have issues with pride, just as the disciples did.

I remember that, when I was younger, we would get into groups to do a task, whether at school or at the youth meeting. There would usually be one person who would have the first idea and then lead the way from there, and with tasks, that is how it has to be. If no one takes the lead, then usually nothing will get done at all. However, I can remember even now that on some occasions I felt resentful, thinking I would have done a better job, even if realistically I knew that the other person had had the best idea and was better at it than me. This is a real pride issue, and we all need to sit on these feelings quickly before they take over and cause problems in our groups of friends. They can quite easily lead to arguments and division!

Remember, we all have gifts. God has given each of us roles to play, but not always to lead. Think of building a house. If we all wanted to be the architect, even if we weren't all good at it, then no house would be built! You need one architect, one quantity surveyor, one project manager, one foreman and many builders. When they work together, the house will get built! I believe that the disciples had understood this and they knew that, by Simon Peter taking the lead, it did not mean he was any more important then they were, but that they had different roles to play. But they were all working together to build God's church.

THE HOLY SPIRIT COMES WITH FIRE

Now look at Acts 2:1–4. These few verses blow me away each time I read them. Can you imagine how unbelievable it must have been to have experienced this? I can guarantee that it would have been better than any special effects you will have seen in a movie.

To me, though, it sounds not only spectacular but also a little scary.

Think about it for a moment. This event did not stay just within the four walls where the disciples were. In verses 5–6 we read that people outside from far and wide heard the sound of the Holy Spirit coming. The crowd that gathered outside the house trying to find out what was going on must have been huge—if you skip to the end of the chapter, you'll see that approximately 3,000 people gave their lives to Christ that day! But I am getting ahead of myself here—let's go back to verses 1–4.

This was no small, insignificant event … it was huge!

Then, once the commotion had died down, these men, many of whom were known not to be educated men but simple folk, walked out speaking in various different recognizable languages—none of which they were able to speak a few hours earlier.

Confession coming up! When I was at school, I struggled with French big time. The teacher we had was really scary and would shout at us quite readily if we got things wrong, which only made me worse. Whenever I read this passage I am so jealous of the disciples, because they did not have to slog away at books to learn a foreign language—it was just given to them. Unfortunately, no person's salvation was dependent on my ability to speak fluent French, so God wisely decided I should learn French the hard way ... but I digress!

WHAT WAS THE POINT OF THE DISCIPLES BEING ABLE TO SPEAK FOREIGN LANGUAGES?

Look at verses 5–12.

- Speaking in these languages was an obvious sign to anyone who didn't know them that something amazingly powerful had been at work, and it would urge them to find out more! Just from the disciples' appearance it must have been obvious to anyone watching that they were mostly uneducated men.

- A special Jewish harvest festival was being celebrated at this time. It was called **Pentecost**, and was also known as the **'Feast of weeks'**. Pentecost marked the fiftieth day after the Sabbath of the Passover week. (And, if you know your Old Testament, you'll remember that **Passover** was the time when they celebrated the angel of death 'passing over' the firstborn of the Jews while they were still slaves in Egypt. Read Exodus chapter 12 to refresh your memory.) There would have been thousands of foreigners visiting Jerusalem during this special festival, all speaking different languages. For them to hear the gospel in their own tongues not only would have been amazing to them, but also would have enabled them to understand the gospel really clearly.

SIMON PETER STEPS UP TO THE PLATE AGAIN!

Look at verses 13–15. It does amaze me that some people

in the crowd actually thought it was a joke and that the disciples were drunk. You may have come across people who have had too much alcohol at various times. I know I have, and alcohol has never caused those people suddenly to become fluent in a foreign language ... incoherent, yes, but definitely not fluent! And how would the crowd have explained the sound of the Holy Spirit's coming that drew them to the disciples in the first place? Their theory really didn't stick!

Simon Peter must have realized that, after this suggestion, now would be a good time to speak to the whole crowd, stop that rumour and explain what was going on.

Note: Look again at verse 14. Simon Peter did not stand up alone, nor did he stand up in front of the disciples, with them forming a sort of backing group. All the disciples were united with Simon Peter. They were quite happy for him to take the lead and speak to the crowd, but they stood up with him, forming a united group.

THE HOLY SPIRIT AT WORK

The Holy Spirit didn't waste any time working in the lives of the disciples, especially in Simon Peter. The following chart shows the many ways in which his character had changed over this period.

Pre-Holy Spirit's arrival

   • Said some really stupid things in response to Jesus; never thought before he spoke and lacked maturity

• Made some boastful claims during the Last Supper about being willing to die for Jesus (which, of course, he wasn't at that time)

• Was fearful of being mocked by others, which was one of the reasons for his denial of Jesus

• Was fearful of death—another reason for his denial of Jesus.

"The Holy Spirit is at work"

Post-Holy Spirit's arrival

• Spoke clearly to the crowd and gave a very mature response to their questioning

• Was not afraid to risk being mocked or worse by the crowd if it turned against him

• Only spoke the truth about Jesus, but did not mince his words. He basically told all the people in the crowd they were responsible for putting to death the Son of God (read verses 23 and 36). This was one very brave man.

So what made the difference?

The Holy Spirit coming with power! He gave Simon Peter wisdom, courage and the words to speak as well as the ability to speak fluently in a foreign language. On his own, he was not able to do these things, but with the Holy Spirit's guidance and power, he was a new man and his mission had begun.

For example: Anyone who knows me would agree that I do not do public speaking. Even in a small group, I find it very hard to express myself, and the thought of standing up in front of hundreds or thousands of people makes me want to hide in the bathroom and lock the door! I am afraid that people will laugh at me or I will get a mental block and forget all I wanted to say. When I was a youth worker, I much preferred talking to our teenagers in very small groups of two or three. To be honest, I would rather work in a sewage plant than work as a lecturer or school teacher.

And yet, when I went to Uganda for a month to work, I found myself speaking at a rally in front of hundreds of people, telling them my story of how I became a Christian. Not only that, but I spoke a few words in their native tongue, risking all sorts of ridicule if I pronounced them badly.

How did I do this?

The answer is simple—I didn't, but the Holy Spirit did! I prayed so hard beforehand, and the Holy Spirit gave me not only the words to say but also the courage to stand up and say them. It was all him and none of me.

Message for today

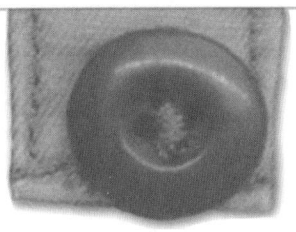

If you have given your life to Jesus, the Holy Spirit is with you, too. He will work in your life in miraculous ways. He will give you courage, strength and wisdom. All you have to do is ask God for help and let yourself be used.

There is no point asking for his help if you then stay locked in your room.

If you are asked to read the Bible at church on a Sunday, go for it, and ask God to give you the courage.

If you have been wanting to ask a friend to come with you to your youth meeting, go for it, and ask God to give you the words to say. Your friend may not give the most positive response at first, but you are being used by God, and who knows whether, later on, this friend might remember what you said and have a change of heart?

Note: Remember that, with Simon Peter, things did not always go well, and he spent a fair amount of time in prison for speaking God's Word—but the Holy Spirit gave him comfort and reassurance and still used him, even in jail, to bring people to Jesus.

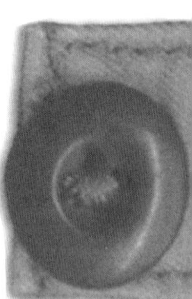

Think tank

1. Imagine you were present when the Holy Spirit first came at Pentecost and you saw and heard all that went on in that room. What do you think your reaction would have been?

2. Do you have an issue with always wanting to lead and not follow? If you do, next time you are in a group when a task is given, try to sit back and let others speak. Let someone else take the lead, and look for the good points in that person's suggestions—don't focus on the bad points.

If, on the other hand, you never speak up in a group because you don't have the courage and you are worried about being teased, ask the Holy Spirit to help you. He gave Simon Peter the courage and the words to say, so he will do the same for you.

Note: Remember that we have all had times when we have tried to speak in public and we feel it all went horribly wrong—we didn't say what we meant to say and are sure no one understood us. My father has been a preacher for over forty years and he still comes away from some services feeling they didn't go well. And yet, nine times out of ten, he will hear later from someone who was at one of those services and find out that God really spoke to him or her through his preaching, or that that person became a Christian through his preaching. If your heart is in the right place and you want to please God, he can use whatever you have to offer for good.

3. This is a hard question, and it may be a good one to bring up as a discussion topic with your leaders when you are next at your youth group.

Do you think God/the Holy Spirit works in dramatic ways today just as he did when he came to the disciples that first time?

If you think the answer is yes, give examples. How do you know that the Holy Spirit was at work at these times, and that it was not the devil trying to deceive? (One key way is to check whether what happens goes against the Bible or not.)

If you think the answer is no, why not?

' . . . Therefore let all Israel be assured of this: God has made this Jesus, whom you crucified, both Lord and Christ. '

(Acts 2 v 36)

 10. **What a difference the Holy Spirit makes!**

(Part 2)

Read Acts 2:14–36

So what did Simon Peter say to the crowd?

In the last chapter, we looked at the run-up to Simon Peter's speech to the crowd, but we didn't actually look at what he said in detail. I have already mentioned that he accused the crowd of putting Jesus to death, but there was more to his speech than just that ... otherwise I think the crowd would have ended up rioting, and that would have been the end of Simon Peter's new career!

Don't be put off by this long passage. His speech can be split up into the following short sections which made compulsive listening for the crowd.

VERSES 14–21

'In these verses, Simon Peter quoted the **prophet** Joel. Remember, a prophet was a person who was told by God what would happen in the future. In the Old Testament, God had told Joel that he would send the Holy Spirit and that his people would experience signs and wonders.

Why did Simon Peter quote the Old Testament? This crowd was made up mainly of devout Jews who would have known their Old Testaments thoroughly. They would have recognized the quote from the book of Joel and hopefully made the link between the prophecy and what had just happened in front of them concerning the disciples. This prophecy had become reality!

VERSES 22-23

The Holy Spirit's coming was only half the picture and Simon Peter now had to bring in Jesus, as it was he who had sent the Holy Spirit in the first place. The crowd knew from the Old Testament that the promised Messiah/Son of God had to come before the Holy Spirit, and yet the people had not accepted that Jesus was the promised Messiah.

So, in these two verses, Simon Peter explained that, although Jesus proved through his miracles that he was the Son of God, they had not accepted him and were responsible for crucifying him. Simon Peter didn't make it easy for them to hear by using subtle language but spelt it out for them by emphasizing the following points:

- He said they 'nailed him to the cross'. The point made here was that Jesus was put to death in the worst possible way. In those times, crucifixion was not only a painful way to go but also a curse. Only the lowest of the low were put to death this way. (Read Galatians 3:13 to back this up.)

- Simon Peter also used the phrase 'you ... put him to death'. In other words, 'you killed him'. It was not a case of just punishment for a crime. Pontius Pilate, the governor at the time of the crucifixion, appealed to the crowd three times to release Jesus as he was innocent, but the crowd would not listen. They murdered him.

(Ouch! That must have really hurt them. These Jews had been waiting for the Messiah for centuries. To suddenly be told they had just killed him must have really hurt—if you look at verse 37, it clearly did!)

But that was not the end of his speech.

VERSES 24–35

Simon Peter now talked about God having raised Jesus from the dead—that he was (and is) alive, and that the disciples were all witnesses to this fact. He quoted King David from the Old Testament. David wrote many of the psalms and in Psalm 16 he had prophesied that the Son of God would not 'see decay'—in other words, he would not remain dead.

It was vitally important for Simon Peter to bring up these Old Testament prophecies that the crowd would have known so well, so that they could see the link between them and the Jesus who had just been crucified.

VERSE 36

Simon Peter ended with an absolutely heart-wrenching sentence that really said it all:

Therefore let all Israel be assured of this: God has made this Jesus, whom you crucified, both Lord and Christ.

In other words, 'You killed the Son of God, the promised Messiah, but he is no longer dead—God has raised him from the dead and he is Lord in heaven.'

WHAT AN AMAZING SPEECH!

Simon Peter could not have composed this speech any better if he had had months to prepare. But this was spontaneous. He could not have known that he would have a captive audience of a few thousand that day, and he did not know that the Holy Spirit was going to come that day.

So how did he do it? He was an uneducated fisherman and yet was able to give a better speech than any American president or English prime minister on the canvassing trail!

Well, I gave you the answer in the last chapter, but here it is again—it was the Holy Spirit at work!

WHAT AN AMAZING REACTION!

Look at verses 37–41. Everyone in the crowd was 'cut to the heart'. In other words, they were distraught. They understood all that Simon Peter had said and believed it wholeheartedly. They were beside themselves at the thought of having been responsible for Jesus's death.

But why had they not believed Jesus's teaching while he was still with them and before he was killed? Why did they suddenly understand now, when they had not understood before?

Again, it was the Holy Spirit at work.

• The people knew their Old Testaments well but had not made the link between the Old Testament prophecies and Jesus. The Holy Spirit was at work opening their eyes to what may seem obvious to some of us with hindsight!

• Look at verse 23 again. It was God's (and Jesus's) 'set purpose' for Jesus to die and rise again. It had to happen like that. He who had never sinned had to take our punishment for our sins and die on the cross. This was the plan that was spoken about in the Old Testament in order for them and all the generations to come (which includes you and me) to have an opportunity to be saved and join him in heaven when we die. The crowd was not supposed to see the link until Jesus's work had been done—and the right time was now ... so their eyes were opened!

Message for today

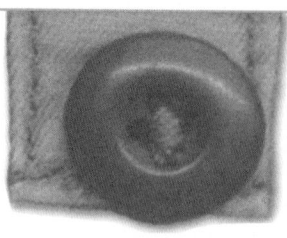

Both Simon Peter and the crowd knew the Old Testament well. All Jews would have learnt the Old Testament religiously, and most Jews today know their Old Testaments so much better than we do. Most Muslims also know the Koran much better than we know the Bible. They quite often put us to shame.

It is vital that we study our Bibles and spend time learning. The Bible is the Word of God and contains all we need to know. And the Holy Spirit shines a light on the Bible and helps us to understand it.

- Without the Holy Spirit, the Bible would just be a history book.

- With the Holy Spirit, the Bible reveals to us the personal love God has for each one of his children and how he has provided a way for us to spend eternity with him. With the Holy Spirit, the Bible becomes more than a history book—it becomes our rescue plan! It comes alive.

For example: Imagine that for your birthday you have just been given an iPod, other MP3 player or whatever is the latest electronic device in town. You know what it is and can admire it straight away. You can read the instructions and understand how it works and how to use it.

However, until you have charged it up, it will not come alive for you. It won't mean an awful lot to you if it just sits on the shelf.

It is the same with the Bible. You can read it and read it, and it seems like just another boring, long book—but once you accept Jesus as your Saviour, the Holy Spirit makes the Bible come alive for you in a way you never imagined.

WHAT A START!

So we leave Simon Peter, having now made a brilliant start to the role that Jesus had intended for him on that first day they met. Simon Peter had been through an awful lot, and there was an awful lot more to come, but I can assure you that he continued to be faithful to God in everything and was a shining example of how God can change someone completely in order to be used by him.

Think tank

1. It is so important that we know the Bible well. It is God's Word that he gave to us. If we ever hope to grow as Christians, and to be able to answer our friends' questions to their satisfaction, we need to study it regularly.

I know that our lives are very busy and it is hard to find time in the day to spend with God, but even just ten minutes a day will help. Just by reading this book right now you are making a start and hopefully learning more about one important character in the Bible's history. Keep it up, even after you have finished this book, and pick another character to learn about.

One important point: Don't just read books about the Bible, though! Read the Bible itself. Remember, Christian books contain different people's opinions on what is written in specific sections of the Bible. You must always read the Bible passages themselves first and check that you agree with what the writer of the Christian book is saying.

For example, there may be some things that I have written that you disagree with, having read the passage in the Bible—that is fine; discuss it among your friends or in your youth group with your youth leaders. All the while, you will be learning more from God's Word.

2. Ask God to help you understand more of the Bible. There are some very difficult passages to understand, but he can help you, through his Holy Spirit, if you ask him. Also, ask older Christians for their opinions and advice. They can be a great help.

3. If you want to continue reading more about Simon Peter's life after Pentecost look at the following chapters from Acts:

Chapter 3, Chapter 4, Chapter 5,

Chapter 10, Chapter 11, Chapter 12.